THE MOST CONVENIENT WAY TO
KEEP TRACK OF CASH PAYMENTS
LOG BOOK

Activinotes

Activinotes

DAILY JOURNALS, PLANNERS, NOTEBOOKS AND OTHER BLANK BOOKS

Copyright 2016

This Book Belongs To

_____

JANUARY

CASH JOURNAL

Reporting period _____

From: _____ To: _____ Balance: _____

Date	Payee	Account	Approved by	Total	Balance

CASH JOURNAL

Reporting period _____

From: _____ To: _____ Balance: _____

Date	Payee	Account	Approved by	Total	Balance

CASH JOURNAL

Reporting period _____

From: _____ To: _____ Balance: _____

Date	Payee	Account	Approved by	Total	Balance

CASH JOURNAL

Reporting period _____

From: _____ To: _____ Balance: _____

Date	Payee	Account	Approved by	Total	Balance

CASH JOURNAL

Reporting period _____

From: _____ To: _____ Balance: _____

Date	Payee	Account	Approved by	Total	Balance

CASH JOURNAL

Reporting period _____

From: _____ To: _____ Balance: _____

Date	Payee	Account	Approved by	Total	Balance

TRACKING LOG

Company Name _____

Total Issued _____   Total Redeemed: _____

Date	No.	Recipient	Authorized by	Amount	Total

TRACKING LOG

Company Name _____

Total Issued _____   Total Redeemed: _____

Date	No.	Recipient	Authorized by	Amount	Total

FEBRUARY

CASH JOURNAL

Reporting period _____

From: _____ To: _____ Balance: _____

Date	Payee	Account	Approved by	Total	Balance

CASH JOURNAL

Reporting period _____

From: _____ To: _____ Balance: _____

Date	Payee	Account	Approved by	Total	Balance

CASH JOURNAL

Reporting period _____

From: _____ To: _____ Balance: _____

Date	Payee	Account	Approved by	Total	Balance

CASH JOURNAL

Reporting period _____

From: _____ To: _____ Balance: _____

Date	Payee	Account	Approved by	Total	Balance

CASH JOURNAL

Reporting period _____

From: _____ To: _____ Balance: _____

Date	Payee	Account	Approved by	Total	Balance

CASH JOURNAL

Reporting period _____

From: _____ To: _____ Balance: _____

Date	Payee	Account	Approved by	Total	Balance

TRACKING LOG

Company Name _____

Total Issued _____   Total Redeemed: _____

Date	No.	Recipient	Authorized by	Amount	Total

TRACKING LOG

Company Name _____

Total Issued _____   Total Redeemed: _____

Date	No.	Recipient	Authorized by	Amount	Total

MARCH

CASH JOURNAL

Reporting period _____

From: _____ To: _____ Balance: _____

Date	Payee	Account	Approved by	Total	Balance

CASH JOURNAL

Reporting period _____

From: _____ To: _____ Balance: _____

Date	Payee	Account	Approved by	Total	Balance

CASH JOURNAL

Reporting period _____

From: _____ To: _____ Balance: _____

Date	Payee	Account	Approved by	Total	Balance

CASH JOURNAL

Reporting period _____

From: _____ To: _____ Balance: _____

Date	Payee	Account	Approved by	Total	Balance

TRACKING LOG

Company Name _____

Total Issued _____   Total Redeemed: _____

Date	No.	Recipient	Authorized by	Amount	Total

TRACKING LOG

Company Name _____

Total Issued _____   Total Redeemed: _____

Date	No.	Recipient	Authorized by	Amount	Total

APRIL

CASH JOURNAL

Reporting period _____

From: _____ To: _____ Balance: _____

Date	Payee	Account	Approved by	Total	Balance

CASH JOURNAL

Reporting period _____

From: _____ To: _____ Balance: _____

Date	Payee	Account	Approved by	Total	Balance

CASH JOURNAL

Reporting period _____

From: _____ To: _____ Balance: _____

Date	Payee	Account	Approved by	Total	Balance

CASH JOURNAL

Reporting period _____

From: _____ To: _____ Balance: _____

Date	Payee	Account	Approved by	Total	Balance

CASH JOURNAL

Reporting period _____

From: _____ To: _____ Balance: _____

Date	Payee	Account	Approved by	Total	Balance

CASH JOURNAL

Reporting period _____

From: _____ To: _____ Balance: _____

Date	Payee	Account	Approved by	Total	Balance

TRACKING LOG

Company Name _____

Total Issued _____ Total Redeemed: _____

Date	No.	Recipient	Authorized by	Amount	Total

TRACKING LOG

Company Name _____

Total Issued _____   Total Redeemed: _____

Date	No.	Recipient	Authorized by	Amount	Total

MAY

CASH JOURNAL

Reporting period _____

From: _____ To: _____ Balance: _____

Date	Payee	Account	Approved by	Total	Balance

CASH JOURNAL

Reporting period _____

From: _____ To: _____ Balance: _____

Date	Payee	Account	Approved by	Total	Balance

CASH JOURNAL

Reporting period _____

From: _____ To: _____ Balance: _____

Date	Payee	Account	Approved by	Total	Balance

CASH JOURNAL

Reporting period _____

From: _____ To: _____ Balance: _____

Date	Payee	Account	Approved by	Total	Balance

CASH JOURNAL

Reporting period _____

From: _____ To: _____ Balance: _____

Date	Payee	Account	Approved by	Total	Balance

CASH JOURNAL

Reporting period _____

From: _____ To: _____ Balance: _____

Date	Payee	Account	Approved by	Total	Balance

TRACKING LOG

Company Name _____

Total Issued _____   Total Redeemed: _____

Date	No.	Recipient	Authorized by	Amount	Total

JUNE

CASH JOURNAL

Reporting period _____

From: _____ To: _____ Balance: _____

Date	Payee	Account	Approved by	Total	Balance

CASH JOURNAL

Reporting period _____

From: _____ To: _____ Balance: _____

Date	Payee	Account	Approved by	Total	Balance

CASH JOURNAL

Reporting period _____

From: _____ To: _____ Balance: _____

Date	Payee	Account	Approved by	Total	Balance

CASH JOURNAL

Reporting period _____

From: _____ To: _____ Balance: _____

Date	Payee	Account	Approved by	Total	Balance

CASH JOURNAL

Reporting period _____

From: _____ To: _____ Balance: _____

Date	Payee	Account	Approved by	Total	Balance

CASH JOURNAL

Reporting period _____

From: _____ To: _____ Balance: _____

Date	Payee	Account	Approved by	Total	Balance

TRACKING LOG

Company Name _____

Total Issued _____ Total Redeemed: _____

Date	No.	Recipient	Authorized by	Amount	Total

JULY

CASH JOURNAL

Reporting period _____

From: _____ To: _____ Balance: _____

Date	Payee	Account	Approved by	Total	Balance

CASH JOURNAL

Reporting period _____

From: _____ To: _____ Balance: _____

Date	Payee	Account	Approved by	Total	Balance

CASH JOURNAL

Reporting period _____

From: _____ To: _____ Balance: _____

Date	Payee	Account	Approved by	Total	Balance

CASH JOURNAL

Reporting period _____

From: _____ To: _____ Balance: _____

Date	Payee	Account	Approved by	Total	Balance

CASH JOURNAL

Reporting period _____

From: _____ To: _____ Balance: _____

Date	Payee	Account	Approved by	Total	Balance

CASH JOURNAL

Reporting period _____

From: _____ To: _____ Balance: _____

Date	Payee	Account	Approved by	Total	Balance

TRACKING LOG

Company Name _____

Total Issued _____   Total Redeemed: _____

Date	No.	Recipient	Authorized by	Amount	Total

AUGUST

CASH JOURNAL

Reporting period _____

From: _____ To: _____ Balance: _____

Date	Payee	Account	Approved by	Total	Balance

CASH JOURNAL

Reporting period _____

From: _____ To: _____ Balance: _____

Date	Payee	Account	Approved by	Total	Balance

CASH JOURNAL

Reporting period _____

From: _____ To: _____ Balance: _____

Date	Payee	Account	Approved by	Total	Balance

CASH JOURNAL

Reporting period _____

From: _____ To: _____ Balance: _____

Date	Payee	Account	Approved by	Total	Balance

CASH JOURNAL

Reporting period _____

From: _____ To: _____ Balance: _____

Date	Payee	Account	Approved by	Total	Balance

CASH JOURNAL

Reporting period _____

From: _____ To: _____ Balance: _____

Date	Payee	Account	Approved by	Total	Balance

TRACKING LOG

Company Name _____

Total Issued _____   Total Redeemed: _____

Date	No.	Recipient	Authorized by	Amount	Total

SEPTEMBER

CASH JOURNAL

Reporting period _____

From: _____ To: _____ Balance: _____

Date	Payee	Account	Approved by	Total	Balance

CASH JOURNAL

Reporting period _____

From: _____ To: _____ Balance: _____

Date	Payee	Account	Approved by	Total	Balance

CASH JOURNAL

Reporting period _____

From: _____ To: _____ Balance: _____

Date	Payee	Account	Approved by	Total	Balance

CASH JOURNAL

Reporting period _____

From: _____ To: _____ Balance: _____

Date	Payee	Account	Approved by	Total	Balance

CASH JOURNAL

Reporting period _____

From: _____ To: _____ Balance: _____

Date	Payee	Account	Approved by	Total	Balance

CASH JOURNAL

Reporting period _____

From: _____ To: _____ Balance: _____

Date	Payee	Account	Approved by	Total	Balance

TRACKING LOG

Company Name _____

Total Issued _____   Total Redeemed: _____

Date	No.	Recipient	Authorized by	Amount	Total

OCTOBER

CASH JOURNAL

Reporting period _____

From: _____ To: _____ Balance: _____

Date	Payee	Account	Approved by	Total	Balance

CASH JOURNAL

Reporting period _____

From: _____ To: _____ Balance: _____

Date	Payee	Account	Approved by	Total	Balance

CASH JOURNAL

Reporting period _____

From: _____ To: _____ Balance: _____

Date	Payee	Account	Approved by	Total	Balance

CASH JOURNAL

Reporting period _____

From: _____ To: _____ Balance: _____

Date	Payee	Account	Approved by	Total	Balance

CASH JOURNAL

Reporting period _____

From: _____ To: _____ Balance: _____

Date	Payee	Account	Approved by	Total	Balance

CASH JOURNAL

Reporting period _____

From: _____ To: _____ Balance: _____

Date	Payee	Account	Approved by	Total	Balance

TRACKING LOG

Company Name _____

Total Issued _____   Total Redeemed: _____

Date	No.	Recipient	Authorized by	Amount	Total

NOVEMBER

CASH JOURNAL

Reporting period _____

From: _____ To: _____ Balance: _____

Date	Payee	Account	Approved by	Total	Balance

CASH JOURNAL

Reporting period _____

From: _____ To: _____ Balance: _____

Date	Payee	Account	Approved by	Total	Balance

CASH JOURNAL

Reporting period _____

From: _____ To: _____ Balance: _____

Date	Payee	Account	Approved by	Total	Balance

CASH JOURNAL

Reporting period _____

From: _____ To: _____ Balance: _____

Date	Payee	Account	Approved by	Total	Balance

CASH JOURNAL

Reporting period _____

From: _____ To: _____ Balance: _____

Date	Payee	Account	Approved by	Total	Balance

CASH JOURNAL

Reporting period _____

From: _____ To: _____ Balance: _____

Date	Payee	Account	Approved by	Total	Balance

TRACKING LOG

Company Name _____

Total Issued _____   Total Redeemed: _____

Date	No.	Recipient	Authorized by	Amount	Total

DECEMBER

CASH JOURNAL

Reporting period _____

From: _____ To: _____ Balance: _____

Date	Payee	Account	Approved by	Total	Balance

CASH JOURNAL

Reporting period _____

From: _____ To: _____ Balance: _____

Date	Payee	Account	Approved by	Total	Balance

CASH JOURNAL

Reporting period _____

From: _____ To: _____ Balance: _____

Date	Payee	Account	Approved by	Total	Balance

CASH JOURNAL

Reporting period _____

From: _____ To: _____ Balance: _____

Date	Payee	Account	Approved by	Total	Balance

CASH JOURNAL

Reporting period _____

From: _____ To: _____ Balance: _____

Date	Payee	Account	Approved by	Total	Balance

CASH JOURNAL

Reporting period _____

From: _____ To: _____ Balance: _____

Date	Payee	Account	Approved by	Total	Balance

TRACKING LOG

Company Name _____

Total Issued _____ Total Redeemed: _____

Date	No.	Recipient	Authorized by	Amount	Total

www.ingramcontent.com/pod-product-compliance
Lightning Source LLC
Chambersburg PA
CBHW081337090426

42737CB00017B/3188